D1565609

CREATION AND THE CONSEQUENCE OF SATAN'S FALL

An exposition of the contoversial "Gap Theory"
as found in Genesis 1:1 and Genesis 1:2

Pieter Dykstra

WestBow
PRESS
A DIVISION OF THOMAS NELSON

Scripture taken from the King James Version of the Bible.

WestBow Press books may be ordered through booksellers or by contacting:

WestBow Press
A Division of Thomas Nelson
1663 Liberty Drive
Bloomington, IN 47403
www.westbowpress.com
1-(866) 928-1240

ISBN: 978-1-4497-5439-6 (sc)
ISBN: 978-1-4497-5440-2 (e)

Library of Congress Control Number: 2012909539

Printed in the United States of America

WestBow Press rev. date: 6/1/2012

Contents

Foreword

In recent history Christianity and the Christian world view have come under increasing attack from the secular world because of its doctrinal stands which are in conflict with secular values and norms.

After the puritan period, secular ideas began to take hold and after the great awakening of the 19th century which brought a lot of spiritual blessings, also spawned numerous non-Christian cults which caused conflict in Christendom and weakened the Christian world view domination, by showing that the Christian world view could be challenged.

Then toward the end of the 19th century with the rise of Darwinism which brought in the theory of evolution, the secular world view rose quickly in prominence and brought pressure on traditional Christian values, to the point where now in the 21st century Christians are considered kooks and extremist.

The rise of evolution, being taught in our classrooms as scientific fact has severely discredited our traditional view of the origin of life and the universe as taught in the Genesis account.

The young earth world view is no longer considered credible, so much so that in recent years Christian

Theologians and Christian scientists have adopted a "Christian" evolution world view by adopting the "Big Bang" theory of creation and instead of a 6, 24 hour day creation week, have come up with 6 ages billions of years in duration, which is nothing more then a Christian version of evolution.

This work explores the various world views and proposes to "bridge" these conflicting views with the "Gap Theory" which claims there was a period of time of unknown duration between **Gen 1:1** and **Gen 1:2.**

This time period, is the source of all the so called "evidence" of evolution.

We hope this controversial subject will clarify and be a blessing to those that are willing to have an open mind to what the scripture is teaching.

The Author

Chapter I

CREATION AND THE CONSEQUENCE OF SATAN'S FALL

The origin of sin has always been attributed to Satan, but what is less clear are the consequences of this sin.

With regard to the origin of sin, we must go to **Isaiah 14:12-17**, which reads

"How art thou fallen from Heaven O Lucifer son of the morning . . . . for thou hast said in thine heart **I will** ascend into Heaven, I will exalt my throne above the stars of God: **I will** sit also upon the mount of the congregation, in the sides of the north: **I will** ascend above the heights of the clouds; **I will** be like the most High"

These are the 5 "I wills" which were the outworking of the sin that was in Satan's heart and manifested itself in these desires of Satan.

But we must go further than that to get at the origin of Satan's sin and for that we must go to **Eziekiel 28:12-17**, which reads:

"Thou sealest up the sum, full of wisdom, and perfect in beauty. Thou hast been in Eden the garden of God; every precious stone was thy covering the sardius, topaz and the diamond, the beryl, the onyx and the jasper, the sapphire, the emerald, and the carbuncle, and gold; the workmanship of thy tabrets and of thy pipes was prepared in thee in the day that thou wast created."

"Thou art the anointed Cherub that covereth; and I have set thee so: thou wast upon the Holy mountain of God; thou hast walked up and down in the midst of the stones of fire."

"Thou wast perfect in thy ways from the day that thou wast created, **till iniquity was found in thee** . . . . and thou hast sinned: thine heart was lifted up because of thy beauty, thou hast corrupted thy wisdom by reason of thy brightness."

There are those who believe that because of the Sovereignty of God and His Omniscience, and the fact that nothing exists that God did not create, that therefore God must have created sin as well. While this concept will undoubtedly be debated for ages to come, in both these passages, Isaiah and Eziekiel there is not a hint of a suggestion that God might have put this in his (Satan's) heart, like in the case of Pharaoh when God said he hardened Pharaoh's heart to show forth his Glory. **(Exodus 10:1)**

Instead we see phrases like "I will" do this and do that, there was nothing but perfection found in him, "thou wast perfect in thy ways from the day that thou wast created, **"<u>till iniquity was found in thee</u>"** and **"<u>Thou hast sinned</u>"**

There is no hint in any of these passages that God was the author of Satan's sin, **<u>sin originated</u>** in Satan, however there does not seem to be an immediate consequence of the sin committed by Satan.

When man committed sin, the penalty was physical and spiritual death **<u>Gen 2:15-17</u>** "And the Lord commanded the man saying, of every tree of the garden thou mayest freely eat: but of the tree of the knowledge of good and evil, thou shalt not eat of it: for in the day that thou eatest thereof thou shalt surely die."

There does not appear to be such consequence for Satan or the other fallen Angels.

There are however, other scriptural references describing negative consequences in the universe and earth as a result of Satan's sin.

The Scripture teaches that creation was perfect until there was iniquity found in the originator of sin, Satan.

These consequences are described in what is called "The Gap theory". In this theory, there is believed to be a gap of time between Gen 1:1 and Gen 1:2 of an undetermined length, the scripture says in **<u>Gen 1:1</u>** "God created the Heavens and the Earth", in **Gen 1:2** there seems to be a change in the physical Universe, and in the Earth in particular, it reads, "And the Earth was without form and void . . ."

The Hebrew word for "was without form" can also be translated "became without form," that is the word "was" can be translated "became".

In other words, in Gen 1:1 God created the physical Universe but then as the result of Satan's sin, the physical Universe appears to have been cursed.

We know from other scripture that the Universe and in particular the Earth is controlled and managed by "Principalities against powers against the rulers of the darkness of this world, against spiritual wickedness in high places" **(Eph 6:12)**, we also know that God has ordained it to be so. In the OT when speaking of these entities He many times calls them "The Prince of Tyre or Persia" etc, in **Dan 12:1** He says "At that time shall Michael stand up, the great Prince which standed for the children of thy people."

Satan himself before he fell was called "The anointed Cherub that covereth."

Satan was a very powerful Angel with high authority given to him by God.

The very fact that he has challenged the authority of God shows that he is still very powerful and it required the sacrifice of God's Son to break that power and will ultimately destroy Satan and send him to the lake of fire.

Resuming again with further evidence for the Gap theory, we find several OT scripture references that could be references to the consequence of Satan's fall.

Jeremiah 4:23 reads: "I beheld the Earth and lo it was without form and void; and the Heavens and they had no light."

Here we have the same description of the earth as in Gen 1:2

Isaiah 24:1 reads "Behold the Lord maketh the earth empty, and maketh it waste, and turned it upside down" and again

Isaiah 24:19,20 "The earth is utterly broken down, the earth is clean dissolved, the earth is moved exceedingly, the earth shall real to and fro like a drunkard and shall be removed like a cottage."

These scriptures seem to hearken back to the description in Gen1:2 where we read "And the earth was (became) without form and void."

Now in all the scripture if there was a consequence of Satan's sin, this (Gen 1:2) is the only reference where there appears to be something out of the ordinary in the space/time continuum.

Time did not start on the first day of creation week, the very first verse in Gen 1:1 says "In the beginning . . . ."

The word beginning denotes time; you can't have a beginning in Eternity and so **after**,

"In the beginning" we read in Gen 1:2 that the earth "Was (became) without form and void . . ."

If the earth was without form and void, it came to be that way after the "beginning".

And so the question might be asked "why", if God created Heaven and Earth, why was it without form and void and remember the Hebrew word for "was" can as easily be translated "became", and so when God created Heaven and Earth, we can assume that this act of creation was perfect and not "without form and void."

We know from subsequent works of creation in the creation week that all the things God created were "behold they were very good." Why then do we have this apparent imperfection right after the creation of Heaven and Earth and **after** the "beginning?" There can be only one reason, **the consequence of Satan's sin.**

In my study of the Gap theory I was always stumped by the objection of the fact that any created creatures in Gen 1:1 like Dinosaurs died, there was death and because of that, the Gap theory was flawed because death came as the result of Adams sin and death was a sign of imperfection, **(Rom 5:12)** but then I realized that the creation in Gen 1:1 was before the creation of Adam and therefore was not subject to the consequence of Adams sin. Only the human race was affected by that. **Romans 5:12** states that "And so death passed upon **all men** . . . ."

Only human beings died because of Adams sin, not the animal kingdom and therefore the death of creatures, (other then those created during the creation week) may have occurred before the creation of man.

The consequence of Satan's sin was not death, because Angelic beings are spirits (Ministering spirits **Heb 1:14**) and spirit beings do not die physically, they are only subject to the second death, the lake of fire. **(Rev 20:14)**

Any death that was among creatures from the Gen 1:1 act of creation was as a result of Satan's sin and it was not the kind of physical death human beings experience as the result of Adams sin, but a universal and instantaneous death which resulted in "the earth was (became) without form and void."

The spirit beings that followed Satan in his sin did not die but according to **2 Peter2:4** "For if God spared not the Angels that sinned, but cast them down to hell and delivered them unto chains of darkness, to be reserved unto judgement" as well as **Jude 6** "And the Angels which kept not their first estate but left their own habitation he has reserved in everlasting chains under darkness unto the judgement of the great day."

These spirit beings are in an intermediate "place of darkness" awaiting judgment day when they will be cast into the lake of fire which is the second death.

The passage in 2 Peter appears to be talking about the Angels that sinned along with Satan after Gen 1:1 but before the creation of man.

The passage in Jude is a reference back to **Gen 6:1-4** where we read "And it came to pass, when men began to multiply on the face of the earth, and daughters were born unto them, that the sons of God saw the daughters of men, that they were fair; and they took them wives of all they chose . . . . There were giants in the earth in those days; and also after that, when the sons of God came in unto the daughters of men, and they bare children to them, the same became mighty men which were of old, men of renown."

If the "Sons of God" mentioned here are in fact Angelic Beings, then we have a clear case of an historical event in which Angels sinned and left their heavenly habitation, came down to earth and married human beings (Women) and had offspring that were different then that which is normally produced by a man and a woman.

Those opposed to the Gap theory, would like us to believe that the account in Gen 6 describes intermarriage between the Godly line (The Sons of God) and the ungodly line (The daughter's of men) which were the descendants of Cain, but this explanation is not supported by the text and the details of the account.

Where else in the scripture are the "sons of God" equated with a "godly line" and why did the marriage between the "sons of God" and the "daughters of men" produce "giants" and why did their "children" become "mighty men which were of old, men of renown?"

Today when a Christian man marries a non-Christian woman, do they produce "giants" or "men of renown" or "mighty men?"

On the contrary, there is nothing unusual about a Christian man marrying a Christian woman, or a non-Christian woman.

WHO THEN ARE THE "SONS OF GOD?"

We do have other scripture references where the term "sons of God" refer to Angels.

Job 1:6 "Now there was a day when the **sons of God** came to present themselves before the Lord and Satan came also among them."

In this verse "the sons of God" can only mean Angels, surely no one would claim that human beings in the form of the "godly line" would present themselves before the Lord, first of all the Lord's dwelling place is in Heaven and human beings did not have access to Heaven. Secondly, the scripture also states that no man shall see the Lord and live.

Therefore the "sons of God" referred to here are Angelic beings.

Job 38:4-7 "Where wast thou when I laid the foundations of the earth? Where upon are the foundations thereof fastened? Or who had laid the cornerstone thereof; when the morning stars sang together, and all the **sons of God** shouted for joy?"

This is a description of what occurred at the Gen 1:1 timeframe and the "sons of God" referred to here are obviously Angels. This also would indicate a time frame before the fall of Satan and the fall of Angels, since there are no signs of disharmony in Heaven, in the <u>Job 38:4-7</u> passage, the "Sons of God" or the Angels "Shouted for joy."

Again scripture abundantly proves that the "sons of God" referred to in Gen 6 are Angels not a godly line of human beings.

And lastly of course the aforementioned **Jude 6** "And the Angels which kept not their first estate, but left their own habitation . . . .", the historical reference as to when this occurred has to be the incident recorded in Gen 6, in all of scripture there is no other reference where and when this occurred, the reference has very specific details like,

The Angels left their first habitation (Heaven) and their first estate (Angels do not marry or are given in marriage) and married human beings (the daughters of men) and had children with them.

Let us elaborate on the nature of the Angels sin in **Jude 6**, and why we believe this applies to the account in **Gen 6:1-4**

Jude 6 reads "And the Angels which kept not their **first estate**", the phrase "first estate" according to the margin in the KJV means "original place with God."

Well, what was their original place with God, was it a location? Or was it a condition or a "lifestyle" so to speak.

In **Luke 20:34-36**, the Lord talks about those that have been resurrected in the afterlife, that they "Neither marry nor are given in marriage, neither can they die anymore:" and then he says that they are like Angels, "for they are equal unto the Angels, in that they "neither marry, nor are given in marriage" and "neither do they die."

The sin of the Angels in **Jude 6** was that they "kept not their first estate" or "original place with God" being the fact that they do not marry or are given in marriage, they sinned and left heaven and married human beings which was recorded in **Gen 6:1-4**

This act was not normal or natural for Angels and Jude goes on to illustrate this by saying in **verse 7** "**Even as** Sodom and Gomorrah and the Cities about them, **in like manner** giving themselves over to fornication and **going after strange flesh** . . ."

In other words, these Angels did "even as" Sodom and Gomorrah, and did something unnatural "in like manner" by "going after strange flesh", being married when it is not natural for an Angel to be married would be considered "going after strange flesh."

We do not need to elaborate on what this "going after strange flesh" in Sodom and Gomorrah meant, suffice it to say that they did something that was unnatural for human beings, just like Angels marrying human women was unnatural for them, they left their "first estate".

The purpose of them doing this was at the behest of Satan and was for the purpose of polluting the human race so that the promised Messiah's, bloodline would be polluted and would no longer be truly human, and it was for this reason, as well as the rampant sin of man, that the flood was send to destroy the human race, so God could start over with Noah and his sons, a pure human race that was not affected by the attempted "biological engineering" of Satan and of which Shem was going to be the one through which the Messiah descended.

To summarize the incident in **Gen 6:1-4** where the "Sons of God" married the "Daughters of men" were in fact the "Angels that sinned and left their habitation and their first estate."

The narrative in Gen 6 is obviously something more then a report on procreation on the part of Godly Mankind, what were people doing up and till the Gen 6 account, were they not marrying each other, and what about after the Gen 6 account, why don't we see any other narratives of people marrying each other.

There was obviously something different happening in the Gen 6 account that was worth mentioning, and the results of these unions, were "Giants", "Mighty men", Men of renown".

Do these descriptions sound like just your everyday ordinary men marrying women and having children?

Even if you hold to the "Sons of God" being the Godly line of human beings, what about before Gen 6, were there only marriages between Godly men and Godly women and ungodly men and ungodly women and then all of a sudden that changed in Gen 6 with the resulting strange offspring?

That explanation just does not make much sense.

The Gap theory therefore is perfectly plausible and has answers for all the difficult questions such as the age of the earth and universe, the obvious existence of pre-historic animals, like Dinosaurs.

While the scientific methods used to date the earth and the universe leave much to be desired, to squeeze the creation of the universe into something like 6000 years ago is difficult to sustain given all the apparent evidence of a much older earth.

The Gap theory has no difficulty supporting a much older earth, since no one knows (and the Bible does not reveal) exactly how much **time** passed between Gen 1:1 and Gen 1:2, it could have been 100's of thousands of years, I personally would not go as far as calling it millions or billions of years, (although the Gap theory has no problem with that either) due to the second law of thermo-dynamics which would place a limit on how old the universe is.

The point is that if there is a gap of time between Gen 1:1 and Gen 1:2 then the length of that time is open for discussion and would be anyone's guess.

And so while the Gap theory supports an older universe and earth, it still and at the same time supports the 6 literal 24 hour day account of creation with the 7th day being a 24 hour literal day of rest, a day on which God rested from all his work.

The Gap theory then has both logical and theological support in the scripture and appears to be in perfect harmony with the notion of an older universe.

Chapter 2

THE ORIGIN OF MANS SIN
AND CONSEQUENCES

One of the reasons we can attribute (or even think about the possibility) consequence to the sin of Satan, is because we have a similar record of mans consequence of sin recorded in the scripture.

Man and the environment in which he existed was perfect and without flaws. In fact, after God created all things and after man had been created in **Gen 1:31** he said about his creation "And God saw everything that he had made, and behold, it was very good."

In other words it was perfect.

His crowning achievement, the creation of man and his companion woman was unique and there was non other creation like it, in **Gen 1:26-28** God said "Let us make man in our image, after our likeness and let them have **dominion** over the fish of the sea and over the foul of the air, and over the cattle, and over all the earth and over every creeping thing that creepeth upon the earth. So God created man in his own image, in the image of God created he him, male and female created he them, and

God blessed them and God said unto them, be fruitful and multiply, and **replenish** the earth, and subdue it and have dominion over the fish of the sea and over the foul of the air, and every living thing that moveth upon the earth."

The word "replenish" the earth appears to indicate something more than just to be "fruitful and multiply."

Why did the Lord choose that word, to "replenish" why not "fill the earth"★ or "occupy the earth."?

★The Hebrew word for replenish can also be translated "to fill", however the point here is that this is not the only way to translate that word, it can also be translated "replenish" as indeed it is rendered "replenish" in the old KJV.

Replenish seems to indicate that the earth was inhabited before, and after the habitation was removed for whatever reason, man was given the task to replenish the habitation.

Could this again be a reference to a previous creation that occurred in Gen 1:1 but was destroyed due to the consequence of Satan's sin in Gen 1:2?

Maybe, maybe not, but mans own sin carried with it consequences of its own.

After the perfect creation of man, God placed them in the Garden of Eden, a perfect environment, with the purpose to "dress it and to keep it."

He also gave man specific instructions as to what he was allowed to do and what not to do.

Gen 2:16,17 says "And the Lord commanded the man saying, of every tree of the garden thou mayest freely eat: but of the tree of the knowledge of good and evil, thou shalt not eat of it: for in the day that thou eatest thereof thou shalt surely die."

And of course we all know the rest of the story, how that God pronounced the fact that it was not good for man to be alone and how God created the woman from one of Adams ribs and how the woman was deceived by the serpent (Satan) and that she and her husband ate the forbidden fruit and that as a result the process of corruption started,

by which both Adam and Eve eventually died physically and that as a result of Adams sin God pronounced a curse on the earth and God said "Cursed is the ground for they sake, in sorrow thou shalt eat of it all the days of thy life; thorns also and thistles shall it bring forth to thee; and thou shalt eat the herb of the field; in the sweat of thy face shalt thou eat bread, till thou return unto the ground; for out of it wast thou taken: for dust thou art and unto dust shalt thou return." **(Gen 3:17-19)**

"Unto Adam also and to his wife did the Lord God make coats of skins, and clothed them." **(Gen 3:21)**

Notice, how that because of Adams sin the first blood (and with it the resulting death of the animal) was shed to provide clothing and covering for Adams sin. Animals had to die that coats of skins could be provided for Adam and Eve. **(Gen 3:21)**

This then was the first "blood sacrifice" for sin, an example set by God Himself to be followed from henceforth, evidence for this is found in the record of a subsequent offering made by Abel and Cain when Abel offered "The firstling of his flock, and of the fat thereof" but "Cain brought of the fruit of the ground an offering unto the Lord." **Gen 4:1-5**

The scripture says "And the Lord had respect unto Abel and to his offering: But unto Cain and his offering He had not respect."

Now why was this? What was the difference?

Abel's offering was a "blood offering" a substitutionary sacrifice, but Cain's offering was the work of his own hands "fruit of the ground" after God had clearly established the requirement of a substitutionary sacrifice.

Heb 11: 4 also refers to this, "By faith Abel offered unto God a more excellent sacrifice than Cain, by which he obtained witness that he was righteous, God testifying of his gifts: and by it being death, yet speaketh." And again "without the shedding of blood there is no forgiveness."

All of this show that the difference between Abel and Cain's offering was faith in a substitutionary sacrifice, which God established back in the Garden of Eden.

MANS EXPULSION FROM
THE GARDEN OF EDEN

In Gen 2:22-24 we find the record of mans expulsion from the Garden of Eden, "And the Lord God said, behold the man is become as one of us, to know good and evil: and now lest he put forth his hand and take also of the tree of life, and eat and live for ever: therefore the Lord God send him forth from the garden of Eden, to till the ground from whence he was taken. So he drove out the man; and he placed at the east of the Garden of Eden Cherubim, and a flaming sword which turned every way, to keep the way of the tree of life."

This by the way was another consequence of Adams sin, expulsion from the Garden of Eden and the active presence of God, could it be that when Satan fell, there was a similar expulsion from heaven and the active presence of God?

Here it is shown that after man had sinned, if God had not driven him out of the garden, man could have partaken of the tree of life in his sinful state and lived forever, in his sinful condition.

This was not God's plan for man. God's plan was to provide salvation, a way out of his sinful condition and back to God after which he would be able to partake of the tree of life and live forever.

Man's sin then came with consequences, namely physical and spiritual death, and because man had been given dominion over God's earthly creation the curse spread throughout creation.

In Romans 8:19-22 we read, "For the earnest expectation of creation waited for the manifestation of the sons of God, for the creature was made subject to vanity, not willingly, but by reason of him who had subjected the same in hope, because creation itself also shall be delivered from the bondage of corruption into the glorious liberty of the children of God. For we know that the whole creation groaneth and travaileth in pain together until now."

God anticipated at the time when he pronounced the curse that he would provide a way of salvation by which the curse someday would be removed.

A footnote here regarding the phrase ". . . waiting for the manifestation of the **"Sons of God"**

Here Christians are referred to as "Sons of God", this does not contradict our previous claim where we stated that the scripture nowhere referred to the godly line as "Sons of God."

The reference "Sons of God" in this verse is purely a N.T. notion, like in **John 1:12** which reads "But as many as received Him, to him gave he power to become the Sons of God" and again in **1 John 3:1-2** where we read, "behold what manner of love the Father hath bestowed upon us, that we should be called the Sons of God" and again in **verse 2** "Beloved now we are we the Sons of

God . . . .", Sons and Daughters of God. Again this was a N.T. notion and was never applied to Godly people in the O.T, in fact when Jesus claimed to be the Son of God, the Jews picked up stones to kill him, why? Because they said by claiming to be the Son of God, He made Himself equal with God.

When Jesus made this claim, He was still living under the O.T. economy and in the O.T. no one claimed to be sons or daughters of God, sons and daughters of Israel or Abraham maybe yes, but not sons or daughters of God. This concept of the Christian being a child of God was purely N.T.

In conclusion, it can be assumed that because of man's fall and with it the far-reaching consequences of this fall, we can equally expect a similar consequence as the result of Satan's fall and the origin of sin itself.

As we have seen, the consequence of man's fall has been revealed in scripture in the Genesis account where we learned that due to man's sin or Adams sin, the penalty of sin, death was passed upon all mankind.

Romans 5:12 states, "Wherefore as by one man sin entered into the world, and death by sin, and so death passed upon all men, for that all have sinned."

In addition to physical and spiritual death, because man had been given dominion over all that God created in the six days of creation week, and because of man's fall, his domain was also affected by his fall, where we read in **Gen 3:17** ". . . Because thou hast hearkened unto the voice of thy wife, and hast eaten of the tree of which I commanded thee, saying thou shalt not eat of it: cursed is the ground for thy sake; in sorrow shalt thou eat of it all the days of thy life; thorns also and thistles shall it bring forth to thee; and thou shalt eat the herb of the field: in the sweat of thy face shalt thou eat bread, till thou return unto the ground; for out of it wast thou taken; for dust thou art, and unto dust thou shalt return."

In addition to the personal curse and consequence upon Adam, we read in **Romans 8:22** "for we know that the whole creation groaneth and travailed in pain together until now."

Now if the consequence of man's sin is death and a curse on man's domain, then it is reasonable to suspect something similar happened as the result and consequence of Satan's original sin and fall.

Just think of it, there was no sin in God's created universe until "iniquity was found in thee." That is in Satan.

Would it not be reasonable to assume that something happened as the result of Satan's fall?

But where do we find such a record in the scripture. Based on my research, the only plausible record is found in Gen 1:2 or the Gap theory where there is believed to be a gap of time between Gen 1:1 and Gen 1:2 An undetermined amount of time, the exact length of which has not been revealed.

EXAMPLES OF SCRIPTURE VERSES
THAT TEACH THE GAP PRINCIPLE

There are those who object to the whole notion of a Gap of time from one verse to the next, or sometimes even within the same verse. They ask what right we have to arbitrarily project an event into the future. This would be a fair question and objection if it wasn't for the fact that we have numerous examples in the scripture of just that, prophesies which were partially fulfilled and the remainder of the same prophetic utterance still unfulfilled.

An easy example is found in **Isaiah 9:6** which reads, "For unto us a child is born, unto us a Son is given, and the government shall be upon His shoulder" We all rejoice and celebrate every Christmas the fact that over 2000 years ago the first portion of the above quoted verse of scripture was literally fulfilled, when Christ the promised Messiah of Israel was born in Bethlehem, but what about the rest of that same verse, ". . . and the government shall be upon His shoulder", this portion of scripture has not been fulfilled yet, but someday it will be literally fulfilled as well, just like the first portion of that verse.

Here is an excellent example of the Gap principle interpretation, this is no theory, it is a historical fact, and when Christ returns, the Government will be on his shoulder, when He will reign for 1000 years over His earthly Millennial Kingdom.

Another example in found in **Zech 9:9-10** where we find a picture of the Messiah riding up to his City "Upon a Colt the foal of an Ass", this was literally fulfilled in AD 33, when Christ rode up to the City of Jerusalem, in fulfillment of this scripture.

The next verse reads "And . . . . He shall speak peace unto the heathen; and His dominion shall be from Sea even to Sea." This scripture too will be literally fulfilled some day, but in the mean time, it has been over 2000 years since the first portion of this scripture was fulfilled, and by the way, when Christ returns, and fulfills this scripture it will be **on the earth** as indicated by the phrase "from Sea even to Sea", there is no Sea in heaven, therefore this scripture is predicting a "Dominion" on the earth, the Millennial Kingdom.

Another example of the Gap principle is set by Christ Himself. Isaiah prophesied in **Isaiah 61:1-2** which reads "The Spirit of the Lord is upon me; because the Lord has anointed me to preach good tidings unto the meek; he hath sent me to bind up the brokenhearted, to proclaim liberty to the captives and the opening of the prison to them that are bound; to proclaim the acceptable year of the Lord, and the day of vengeance of our God."

In **Luke 4:16-21** the Lord Jesus Christ quoted this scripture, but when he had finished the clause" . . . to proclaim the acceptable year of the Lord", he closed the book and said "This day is this scripture **fulfilled** in your ears."

What makes this so unusual is that he stopped at a comma! Why did He stop at that point of that portion of scripture?

Because the next clause "And the day of vengeance of our God", was not to be fulfilled for over 2000 years and is still future.

The Lord Himself, the Master interpreter of Holy Scripture laid down the principle of a Gap interpretation, He said that "today", that is 2000 years ago "this scripture is fulfilled in your ears." Why? Because this portion of scripture was talking about Him, the Messiah who was to do exactly what this prophesy predicted of Him, 2000 years ago.

He did not quote the last portion of this passage because the time for "The day of vengeance of our God" had not yet come, it was still future. Christ here as the Master interpreter laid down the rule for the Gap interpretation principle.

The Apostle Peter also spoke of the Gap principle in **1 Peter 1:10-11** which reads, "Of which salvation the Prophets have inquired and searched diligently, who prophesied of the grace that should come unto you, searching what or what manor of **time,** the Spirit of Christ which was in them did signify, when it testified beforehand the sufferings of Christ and the Glory that should follow."

These Prophets prophesied many times in the same verse of scripture, both the sufferings and the Glory of Christ, which were pictures of the first and second coming, and even though the glorious part has not yet been fulfilled, the literal sufferings occurred over 2000 years ago, when Christ died on the cross for our salvation. The Prophets saw these two events as two peaks of a mountain, but what they failed to see at the time when they uttered their prophesies, were the valleys of time in between these peaks.

From their vantage point the sufferings and glories of the Messiah occurred at the same time, but from our vantage point we know that the sufferings occurred over 2000 years ago, establishing again the Gap principle.

The old and new testaments give ample proof of the truthfulness and plausibility of a gap of time separating one verse of scripture from another, even though at the time of the writing of a given text the Prophet does not know the significance of what he is prophesying, and most of the time when given sufficient time the truth becomes clear.

We have this assurance, that if the first portion of the prophesy was fulfilled literally, **we can know** for sure that the second halve of the prophesy will come to pass as well, literally, and as such there is no **Prima Face** reason to deny the truth and reality of there being a Gap of time of unknown duration between Gen 1:1 and Gen 1:2.

There are many more examples of this truth in the Bible, but these 4 examples will suffice.

One more point about the fulfillment of Prophesy, as a general rule, if the first part of the prophesy is fulfilled **literally,** then the second part of the prophesy will be fulfilled **literally** as well, if the first coming of Christ to the earth was a **literal** coming, then the second coming of Christ to the earth will be **literal** as well.

In the phrase "And the earth was (became) without form and void and darkness was upon the face of the deep . . ." **(Gen 1:2a)**

If this is not the result of Satan's fall, then why was there this apparent imperfection? If we admit that this description of the creation was somewhat other then perfection, then what was the cause?

To turn it around and put it another way is this, if Gen 1:2 is not a description of the consequence of Satan's fall, then where in all the scripture might there be evidence of this event that can be found.

We have already concluded that because of the example we have in the scripture of the consequence of man's sin, it is reasonable to expect to see a similar consequence of Satan's fall and sin in the scripture, the question then becomes where.

I realize that this whole argument comes dangerously close to "begging the question", but the fact that there is this looming question deserving an answer, does not allow us to just ignore it, and if there is an answer in the scripture the only scripture that comes to mind is the apparent chaos in Gen 1:2.

We have scripture that shows Satan to be the originator of sin, but there is no scripture that shows the consequence of Satan's sin. If we say there was no consequence then why was there a consequence as the result of man's fall and sin. It is logical to assume Satan's fall would have similar consequences. And if Satan's fall did have consequence, then the only plausible scripture in which this is revealed is Gen 1:2

WHERE DID DINOSAURS COME FROM AND WHAT HAPPENED TO THEM

There is no escaping this dilemma, if we couple this with the fossil evidence we have of the existence of Dinosaurs and a much older universe then 6000 years and the apparent problem we are faced with trying to account for the presence of Dinosaurs in the ark and lack of subsequent history of these creatures living on the earth and becoming extinct. (Notwithstanding some gallant efforts to find them in such bible books as Job etc)

The sheets simply do not fit the bed.

On the other hand if Dinosaurs were part of the original creation in Gen 1:1 and they became extinct due to the fall of Satan, then that would explain a lot.

One additional observation regarding the chronology of the creation account in Genesis needs to be made.

One of the reasons, if not the only reason there are those that believe in a 6000 year young earth and universe, is because they read Gen 1:1 as follows: "In the **beginning** God created the Heavens and the Earth." They then proceed with verses 2, 3, 4 and 5 which brings us to the beginning and end of the first day.

After this they continue with the second, third, fourth, fifth and sixth day (the day God created Adam) and for some reason lump them all together as if, the entire creation process, starting with the creation of the Heavens and the Earth up until the sixth day, were a seamless chronology with no break at all.

In other words we see the duration of this entire process as consuming 6, 24 hour periods of time, and we say that God created the Heavens and the Earth including the universe, light, day, night, the firmament, the oceans,(seas) the dry land, vegetation and tree life, the sun, the moon, the stars, all the life forms in the oceans, birds, all cattle beasts and creeping things and finally Man and that He did **all** of this in 6, 24 hour days.

We then through an elaborate process of calculating the average lifespan of mankind before the flood as well as the generations after the flood, and we conclude that this whole process lasted approximately 6000 years.

The only problem with this reasoning is that the Bible text does not support such a conclusion.

Nowhere in the creation account does the Bible say that the creation part in Gen 1:1 where God created the heaven and the earth was part of the 6 day creation week, at which time He created all the rest of the earths created Beings, time and matter. Nowhere in the text are we led to believe that this was all one and the same process and chronology.

The truth is that in Gen 1:1 "In the beginning God created the Heavens and the Earth" **Period!**

This initial act of creation had nothing to do with what happened after that, and it can be assumed just as easily that an undetermined amount of time passed before God created all that He made during the 6 day creation week.

The natural reading of the text is that there was a creative act in Gen 1:1 and then **after** that, God proceeded with the activity recorded in the rest of the verses in Genesis chapter 1.

And so maybe the 6 days of creation and subsequent human procreation may have lasted 6000 years, it does **not** mean that this included the act of creation in Gen 1:1.

And therefore the natural reading of the text in the Genesis account fits the possibility of an old earth scenario.

THE ORIGIN OF DEMONS, WHERE DID THEY COME FROM

In addition to the problem of an apparent older universe, the existence of pre-historic animals and the lack of historic evidence of their existence and extinction after the flood, we also have the problem of the origin of Demons, where did they come from.

We know that Angels were created by God "In the beginning . . . ." Gen 1:1 we even have scripture talking about the nature and classification if Angels. We know that they are a "company" and not a "race." We know that they neither marry nor are given in marriage, and neither do they die. (**Luke 20:34-36**)

Some different classifications of Angels are: **General Angels,** the ones that are "messengers" and protectors of the "heirs of salvation."

There are the **Cherubim,** the word Cherubim means to cover or to guard. Satan was a Cherub before his fall. (**Eziekiel 28: 14-16**)

The **Seraphim,** this class of Angels are in charge of acceptable Worship and Holiness in the service of God.

The Archangels, such as Michael and Gabriel who represent peoples, like Michael is the Prince of the people of Israel and Gabriel was used to announce great events, like the birth of Christ and the announcement of the birth of John the Baptist.

There are good Angels and evil Angels, the Bible says that some of the evil Angels are kept in prison (**2 Peter 2:4 and Jude 6**) and some are still free (**Ps 78:49 ; Rom 8:38 ; 1 Cor 6:3**) and of course Satan who is "Roaming about like a roaring Lion seeking whom he may devour." (**1 Peter 5:8**)

And then the Bible speaks of Demons, the term Demon in the NT for the most part refers to evil spirits. The origin of Demons however is somewhat of a perplexing question. In general there are 3 explanations suggested:

1) **They are the souls of bad men.** This is the view of Philo, Josephus and practically all of the early Christian writers. We object because the scripture everywhere represents the unsaved dead as being in Sheol and Hades and not as roaming around the earth. (**Ps 9:17 ; Eziek 32:17-24 ; Luke 16:23)**

2) **That they are fallen Angels** which are not confined to Tartarus (**Dan 10:13, 20; Rev 12: 7, 9**) this is the traditional view and there is a lot of support for it. But there are two things that are perplexing regarding this theory, a) It is never shown that a fallen Angel ever sought embodiment in a human being, and b) It seems incongruous to say that a man was possessed by a fallen Angel which we should be able to say if

fallen Angels and Demons are one and the same thing.

3) **That they are the disembodied spirits of a pre-Adamic race.** This view has against it the fact that the scriptures nowhere speak of such a race. But since the fall of Satan, his Angels and the Demons must have taken place somewhere between **Gen 1:1 and Gen 1:2.** It is not improbable that in addition to Angels, there was a race or company of beings that inhabited the earth over whom Satan ruled and who also fell when he fell. Or maybe they were just a company of beings which God had created to inhabit the earth before the catastrophe of Gen 1:2, and as their punishment God allows them to be about in a disembodied state until their judgement and then cast into the lake of fire which is the second death. Several writers have espoused this view, like Pember, Ottman and Pardington.

In **Matt 8: 28,29** there is a very interesting account of Jesus casting out Demons out of 2 citizens from the country of the Gergesenes, the passage says that the Demons spoke to Jesus and it says in **verse 29,** "And behold, they cried out, saying, what have we to do with thee, Jesus thou Son of God? Art thou come hither to torment us **before the time?"** What time were they talking about? The time the Demons apparently know is the time of their final judgement and that time had not yet come. And how did they know about this judgement time? Was it perhaps the time that God had told them about when He pronounced judgment on them at the time that they sinned way back in Gen 1:2, in similar fashion as when He pronounced judgment on Man after he sinned?

This view in #3 supports the fact that Demons seek re-embodiment.

Also the destruction described in **2 Peter 3:5,6,** (Which reads "For this they willingly are ignorant of that by the word of God the Heavens were of old, and the earth standing out of the water and in the water: whereby **the world that then was**, being overflowed with water, perished:") could refer to a judgement upon such a pre-Adamic race whereby God's perfect creation was changed into the chaos of Gen 1:2, and just like the Human race is faced with the consequence of Adams sin, maybe in like fashion the race that God had created to inhabit the earth in Gen 1:1 had to deal with and was affected by the sin and consequence of Satan's fall, especially if the pre-Adamic race was part of Satan's "dominion" and Satan's fall had a consequence on his "dominion" just like Man's fall had a consequence on Man's dominion, the earth.

All of this would support the notion that when God in **Gen 1:28** gave the "new" human race the commission to "replenish the earth" He in fact had re-created the earth to adapt it for a new race to complete what he had intended originally in the creation of Gen 1:1

This would also explain the fact that after God had given the new earth to be Man's "domain," that after Man sinned his domain was cursed, lost and given back to Satan whose domain it was originally.

Proof of this is found in the following scripture texts. The temptation of Christ by Satan in **Matt 4:1–11** in this narrative the Holy Spirit leads Jesus into the wilderness and after he fasted 40 days and 40 nights, Satan came and tempted Him in 3 areas, His physical needs, He was hungry (**vs. 3 and 4**) His presumptive needs, where the Devil tried to have Him test God the Father (**vs.5–7**) and by the way Satan knows the scriptures, he quoted **Psalm 91:11, 12** to the Lord.

And lastly he tempted Him with pride and covetness when he (Satan) said in **vs 8 and** 9 "Again, the Devil taketh Him up into an exceedingly high mountain, and showeth Him all the Kingdoms of the world, and the Glory of them and said unto Him, all these things I will give thee, if thou wilt fall down and worship me."

We know of course the outcome of that temptation, when the Lord rebuked Satan and said "Get thee hence Satan, for it is written, thou shalt worship the Lord thy God, and Him only shalt thou serve."

There are a couple of observations of this particular temptation.

1) In this temptation, Satan in effect was auditioning the Lord Jesus Christ for the position of the "Antichrist", what Satan offered the Lord, is exactly what he will give to the Antichrist at the end time, when the Antichrist will be revealed and will rule the whole world during the tribulation period.

2) And this is the point that pertains to the notion that Satan has usurped the dominion of the earth from Adam and is presently the ruler of this world.

When Satan made the offer to Christ, the Lord did not say wait a minute, what you are offering me is not yours to give.

No, Christ knew that because of Adams fall, the dominion of the earth had reverted back to Satan, who's dominion we believe it was back in Gen 1:1, until it was given to Adam by God when he said in **Gen 1:26–28** ". . . . God said unto them . . . . be fruitful and multiply and replenish the earth, and subdue it and have **dominion** over the fish of the sea and over the fowl of the air and every living thing that moveth upon the earth" Christ did not dispute the claim of Satan, that he (Satan) had the right and power to give all that he wanted to give to whomever he wanted to give it.

Paul also said that Satan was the "God of this world" and the head of all the, "Principalities and Power in high places."

And so it is an undisputed fact that Satan is the ruler of this world since he received it when Adam sinned and this will remain to be the case until Christ returns and takes it back and rules as "King of Kings and Lord of Lords." **Rev 19:16**

The very fact that the earth's domain was given to Satan after the fall of man, stirs up all kinds of questions of "why?"

Maybe the fact that because of the fall of Satan, God decided to finally and forever deal with sin in the universe, by re-creating the earth and by creating man in his own image (this was unique He had never done this before, none of the Angelic beings were created in His image and there was no way of salvation for any other creature then man) Man was unique, created in Gods image with a free will to choose between good and evil in an environment uniquely adapted to him where God put him to the test, which of course he failed but the difference this time(as opposed to the fall of Satan and the Angels) was the fact that God implemented a plan of salvation for man. Ultimately this would not only save those human beings that accepted His free gift of salvation but **in the process destroy Satan and eradicate sin from Gods universe.**

If this speculation is truth then the Gap between Gen 1:1 and Gen 1:2 is no longer a **theory** but becomes a philosophical and theological **necessity** like one of Gods decrees, because in this decree it paves the way in order for God to deal with sin once and for all.

All of this of course is conjecture since the scripture nowhere gives direct testimony of these events.

But the scripture is not completely silent on the subject. We have little tidbits of information here and there, information that was given by God for the purpose of examination and then by the use of the God given faculty of reason and the guidance of the Holy Spirit to try to reconstruct what happened.

After all is it not God who says in his word "Come and let us reason together . . ." And again "When the Spirit of truth has come; He will guide you into **all** truth . . ."

Who is to say that the Gap theory is not part of this guidance into all truth?

The test of any reasoning like this should be "does this give glory and honor to God, or does it detract from what scripture has revealed about Gods purpose, sovereignty, and glory."

We must conclude that this hypothesis does not detract but adds to Gods purpose, sovereignty, glory, and the fact that such revelation as received from the apparent imperfection in the creation account of Gen 1:2 invites investigation and should be explored.

Chapter 3

WHAT EFFECT WILL THE GAP THEORY HAVE ON THE CHRISTIAN WORLD VIEW

The preceding hypothesis of the Gap Theory makes for an interesting read. But beyond that, does it have any real impact on the Christian life. Does it affect our world view and is it relevant. I believe the answer to these questions is a resounding yes, it does make a difference and it is relevant. If the Gap Theory and its conclusions are in fact true and a correct interpretation of the clues revealed in scripture, then that means God has revealed relevant truth about the origin of the universe.

We also know that when God reveals truth, that His truth always has a purpose.

And so we ask, what is the purpose of revealing this information regarding the origin of the universe. Truth is truth; we can not postulate theories about the origin of the universe unless we are grounded in truth.

If we look around, we see scientific theories such as the theory of evolution, which is diametrically opposed to the Genesis account of the origin of the universe.

The Genesis account claims that God **created** out of nothing, and evolution claims that matter **evolved** into the current state of complexity. The main reason the scientific community has abandoned the creation account is because on the surface it appears to teach that God created the universe approximately 6000 years ago and modern science observing the evidence of the age of the earth, has concluded that the earth and the universe is much older. They look at fossil evidence and the different strata levels of the earth and conclude that the age of the earth must be much older.

They use questionable carbon dating methods to determine the age of the earth and their findings they believe do not square with the Genesis account. So much so that, Christian Theologians and Christian scientist are now re-examining the creation account and have concluded that maybe the six day creation week in Genesis are really 6 separate ages, millions of years in duration in which God created what is described as an evolutionary process with a Christian spin on it.

Again, why? Because a 6000 year old earth is not plausible.

And so the result of this is that in today's Christian world view, we are divided into 2 camps, 1) The traditional view of a 6000 year old earth with 6 literal 24 hour days of creation and 2) The more modern view of the "Big Bang" creation of the universe, in which the universe and the earth evolved through a "sanctified" process of evolution, whereby God used millions and billions of years to "create" the current state of matter.

The result?

The first world view is being ridiculed by the scientific community and the second world view is being ridiculed by most of Christendom.

All of this, the capitulation of the "Big Bang" Christian world view to the atheistic view of evolution is all so unnecessary, if the Gap Theory was adopted.

The reason evolution is wrong, and the "Big Bang" creation view is wrong, and for that matter the Christian 6000 year old earth view is wrong, is because none of these views are grounded in the truth.

They all use the wrong premises when all along God is saying, why are you doing this, when the scripture clearly reveals that there is a gap of time between Gen 1:1 and Gen 1:2, and this gap of time is the source of the "evidence" which the scientific community has attributed to "evolution."

Our God is not so small that he would need a "Big Bang" and an evolutionary process to "create" the current universe.

Our God is the God Who created something out of nothing, He simply spoke the Word (Jesus Christ the Word or Logos of God) and the universe came into being instantaneously, by Fiat.

God does not need millions of years to accomplish his purpose, our God is the Lord God Almighty, and there is nothing too hard for Him.

Up until recent history, the only Christian view of creation was the 6000 year old earth view.

It was not until evolution around the turn of the previous century began its ascent, (the writings of Darwin and the monkey trial) that Christians began feeling the pressure from the scientific world and they began to rethink their view of the creation account. All of a sudden they were faced with "evidence" of a 13.3 billion year old universe, of the Neanderthal man and several other phases of man supposedly evolving from a monkey, that they felt a need to change their ridged stand on the misunderstood Genesis account of creation.

And so they capitulated and came up with their own scheme of "Christian" evolution by adopting the "Big Bang" theory of the origin of the universe and changing the six 24 hour days of the creation week into 6 ages of time, which is nothing more then evolution with a Christian spin or flavor. It is sad to see part of the Christian community falling away from the true Christian teaching on the origin of the universe. And so we have an ongoing struggle between the young earth and the old earth points of view. We believe that as a result of the revelation of the truth of the Gap Theory, there is a way out of this dilemma.

Chapter 4

PRACTICLE APPLICATION
OF THE GAP THEORY

As Christians we do not have to capitulate to the ungodly world view of evolution.

When are we going to learn that becoming like the world, will never earn us credibility and will **not** earn us the right to be heard.

It is this kind of failure on the part of the Christian world view that makes the skeptic smile and re-enforces his believe that Christianity does not have the answers to the mystery of the origin of life nor the answer for the origin of the universe. When we compromise ourselves and dabble in a "Christian" version of evolution, we not only discredit God, but we misrepresent God and the creation account, which has been clearly revealed in the scripture.

When we allow scripture to speak for itself, without a cloud of interpretational confusion, which purports the scripture to say something which it clearly does not, then the scripture will report the truth, because it can not and will not lie. When we insist on a 6000 year old universe,

I respectfully believe that we misrepresent the record of the origin of the universe as it is recorded in the Genesis account.

When we insist on a "Big Bang" version of the creation of the universe, I again respectfully believe that we misrepresent what scripture has recorded regarding the creation of the universe. God in time and space has spoken through nature by way of General revelation and through the Bible by way of Special revelation.

Whether we like it or not, General Revelation, through the external evidence all around us, leads us to the conclusion, that there is abundant evidence for an "Old" universe.

When we look at space, and especially now in the 21st century after man has ventured into the realm of space through the efforts of a worldwide space exploration program, and we look at the stars and the millions of Galaxies, it is difficult to believe that all of this came into being a mere 6000 years ago.

We measure distances in space in terms of light years.

We now know how fast light travels, which we call the speed of light, and when we measure how far light can travel at the speed of light for a year; we arrive at the unit of measurement called a light year.

When we look at the distant Galaxies and estimate how far these Galaxies are away from the earth, we realize that the time it took light to travel from the distant

Galaxies to reach the earth, can only be measured in staggering numbers of light years. I have always looked at the estimates put forth by the scientific community of millions and billions of light years as not being very credible, because they present them as a matter of fact, when in reality all they are doing is "guessing", if they would say that they were guessing, I guess (pardon the pun) I would be more inclined to hear what they claimed, but they present this data as scientific fact. But the way I see it is that we really do not need to speculate in terms of millions and billions of light years, all we need to do is to realize that it took longer then 6000 years for that light to reach the earth in order to see that the external evidence does not match our 6000 year old earth theory.

When we look at the immensity of the universe, we realize how small we are and 6000 years somehow does not "feel" adequate. The "measuring stick" of a 6000 year old universe does not seem to be up to the task. And before you tell me how that "feelings" have nothing to do with what we believe about what God has declared to be the truth; and how we don't believe something which God has revealed just because it does or doesn't "feel" right.

My answer to that is, "you are absolutely right."

My contention is not with what God has revealed, my contention is with what God has **not** revealed. I do not believe that God has revealed either in General or Special revelation that the earth is only 6000 years old. Some of us have interpreted it that way but that does not make it true. Many centuries ago men believed that the earth was flat and that the Sun revolved around the earth, this believe was supported by the Church and contemporary Theologians of that day. Well we now know that, that believe was erroneous and wrong and we now know and believe that the Earth is round and that the Sun does not revolve around the Earth, a clear cut case that shows that the "interpreters" of scripture were wrong and that the scripture was right all along.

When we add to this the Special revelation which we can glean from the Bible, we realize that the Bible if allowed to speak for itself, without the prism of human "interpretations" will point to the unmistakable fact that the earth is much older then 6000 years and that the Biblical account is open to the concept of an "old" universe.

We spoke earlier in this work about how certain assumptions made about the Genesis account of creation were not necessarily true. We spoke about how some interpreters lump together as one continuous chronology, Gen 1:1 where we read "In the beginning God created the Heavens and the Earth" **followed** by the 6, 24 hour days of creation, in which God created light, day, night, the firmament, the oceans, (seas) the dry land, vegetation and tree life, the Sun, the Moon, the Stars, all life forms in the oceans, birds, all cattle, beasts, and creeping things and finally man, after which they calculate the lifespan of human beings before the flood as well as the generations after the flood and then proclaim that all of this took a total of 6000 years to complete. We also noted that the scripture text does not support such a conclusion. When reading the creation account, it clearly states that there was an act of creation in Gen 1:1 at which **time** God "Created the Heavens and the Earth" After this the natural reading of the text shows there were other things and events which occurred **before** the 6, 24 hour day acts of creation commenced. But because of what the late great Bible teacher Dr Alva McClain (In his work "Daniels prophesy of the 70 weeks") called our western thirst for chronological unfolding of events, where we are always looking for the next event on the chronological timetable, we simply assumed that the 6 days of the creation week, chronologically followed the events from Gen 1:1, 2 and 3. When in fact the reading of the text does **not** support that, and even though this work is about the "Gap Theory" where we believe there was a gap of time between Gen 1:1 and Gen1:2 due to the consequence of Satan's fall, we believe that even without that specific event, the natural reading of the text would still demand an interruption of the chronology of time between Gen 1:1 and the commencement of the 6, 24 hour day creation week.

The way out of this dilemma is to simply adopt and embrace the truth of the "Gap Theory" It will eliminate the need to "dabble" in the dangerous and Godless theory of evolution, even one with a "Christian" spin on it, and we can abandon the 6000 year old (young) universe theory, a theory that in the light of modern day general revelation is simply not credible or sustainable. Again if we allow the scripture to speak for itself, and if we inject the proffered Consequence of Satan's fall, we arrive at the following chronology of the origin of the universe:

1) **Eternity past.** The condition before God created anything and where there was perfect harmony and unity in the God-Head. God the Father, God the Son or the Word/Logos and God the Holy Spirit dwelt together in perfect love, perfect harmony, perfect unity and perfect communion. It was in this condition that the Bible speaks of the God-Head planning the creation of all things, including the Angelic Host, Mankind and the Plan of Salvation. We do not know in depth as to why God decided to create, but we do know that it was not because God was lonely (as some preachers erroneously proclaim) and wanted companionship, because the Tri-une God-Head already experienced perfect love and communion within the God-Head, we also know very little about the purpose of creation, we read in **Rev 4:11** that "Thou art worthy o Lord, to receive Glory and Honor and Power: for Thou hast created all things and **for Thy pleasure they are and were created."**

2) **Gen 1:1 "In the beginning God created the heavens and the earth"** This is the record where God **created** something **out of nothing**, the word used for "created" is the Hebrew word "Bara" which basically means the bringing into existence substance, out of nothing or creation by Fiat. This was not rearranging existing matter from one form to another form; this was speaking something into existence, where there was nothing to begin with. This was also the beginning of time, before this act of creation there "is" (we can't say "was" in this context) eternity "past" which again

is a word that belongs in a time/space continuum and not in the eternal concept, and even the word "concept" is not appropriate when discussing eternity. Again **Gen 1:1** is the beginning of time and the beginning of the universe, "Heavens and Earth" is the origin of all physical matter and anti-matter and beyond that it is the origin of all the Angelic Host, all the Angels including Lucifer (Later to be known as Satan) had their origin in **Gen 1:1**. Again this was God creating all things visible and invisible. **Hebrews 11:3** "By faith we understand that the worlds were framed by the Word of God, so that the things which are seen were not made of the things that are visible" **John 1:1-3** "In the beginning was the Word, and the Word was with God, and the Word was God, He was in the beginning with God, **all** things were made through Him, and without Him nothing was made that was made." The earth was also made at that time frame, and when God created (Bara) all things it was not the result of some kind of "Big Bang", God simply spoke and it was done (Fiat), this whole notion of a "Big Bang" came to be because of the theory of evolution which needed something, anything, other the concept of a God creating something out of nothing, and unfortunately the "Christian" "Big Bang" theory has adopted that as well.

3) **Gen 1:2a "The earth was (became) without form, and void; and darkness was upon the face of the deep . . ."** Here is where we believe something happened to the perfectly created earth in Gen 1:1. The earth created in Gen 1:1 was

not imperfect, the text says "In the beginning God created the Heavens and the Earth." There is no indication at all that there was something imperfect in the created earth. Now there are those that interpret the description of the earth in Gen 1:2a as being a description of what the earth was like "In the beginning". They say that when God created the earth in Gen 1:1 He created it "Without form and void; and darkness was upon the face of the deep" and that after that he "fine-tuned" the earth in Gen 1:2b and Gen 1:3 into what the earth became to be, as we know it now, today. This attempt to avoid the implication of having to accept the "Gap Theory" creates all kinds of new problems for them, a) This make God the author and creator of imperfection, where else did God create something that required "fine-tuning" after he created it initially, b) This makes God the creator of "darkness", God is Light, in Him is no darkness at all, this is as can be plainly seen, an attempt to sidestep the obvious evidence of the Gap Theory, they make God the creator of chaos and the creator of darkness. To me it takes a greater leap of faith to believe that, then the Gap Theory itself. **First** of all, the phrase in Gen 1:2a where it reads "The earth was without form and void," the word "was" can also be translated as "became" and so if we translate it using that word, the passage translates as follows: "The earth **became** without form and void." If this translation be allowed, it completely changes the meaning of the text. It would change the perfect earth of Gen 1:1, into something imperfect in Gen 1:2a.

Secondly if the word "Became without form and void" is used then **this indicates a period of time** between when the earth was created perfect in Gen 1:1 and when it became "Without form and void" in Gen 1:2a. The question then becomes **how much time,** the answer is we don't know, the Bible simple does not reveal specifically how much time passed between Gen 1:1 and Gen 1:2, we just know that there is a gap of time between the 2 points. **Thirdly** why was there this change of the earths condition between Gen 1:1 and Gen 1:2a, the answer we believe is **the consequence of Satan's fall**, Satan was created perfect in the beginning, until "Iniquity was found in thee," we do not know **when** Satan fell, we just know from the scripture that he did and we can assume that there were consequences as the result of his fall and we believe that part of these consequences was the change in the earths condition, it "Became without form and void, and **darkness** was upon the face of the deep." Throughout scripture "Darkness" has always been as a result of sin, for example because of Gods salvation we have been "Translated out of darkness, into His marvelous light." And so the "darkness upon the face of the deep," we believe was the result of Satan's sin.

4) **Gen 1:2b "And the Spirit of God moved upon the face of the waters" Gen 1:3 "And God said, let there be light, and there was light"** Light and darkness are very powerful symbolic signs of sin and righteousness, while in these verses there obviously were physical

changes brought about in the earth, this was also a very powerful picture of the result of Satan's sin (darkness) and the righteousness of God who brought about changes in the spoiled earths condition, by bringing about a re-creation in the earth in order to restore it back to its original condition of Gen 1:1. **In Gen 1:4** "and God saw the light, that it was good, and God divided the light from the darkness."

5) **Gen 1:5-31** starting at verse 5, God started the six 24 hour day creation week at which time He created and in a sense re-created the earth and all the things that are in them, including Man whom he created in his own image. The re-creation of the earth should not be considered something strange, the scripture tells us that sometime in the future God will make "a new Heaven and a new earth." and in Rev 21 John the Revelator wrote "And I saw a new heaven and a new earth" in which God so drastically re-created the earth that it says there was no longer a need for the sea's or the sun and the moon because God will be the light thereof.

And so **to recap**, in **Gen 1:1** "God created the Heavens and the Earth" which was the origin of the earth.

The universe and the earth did not evolve over billions of years, but was created out of nothing, and if we are to believe the scientific "speculation," this would have occurred approximately 13.3 billion years ago. The universe and the earth existed in the form God had created them in Gen 1:1 until the fall of Satan, which caused a curse on the universe and on the earth in particular and the earth was changed, it became "without form and void, and darkness was upon the face of the deep" After this catastrophic event, and we don't know how long after, God re-created the earth with all that is therein, like light, day, night, the firmament, the oceans, (seas) the dry land, vegetation and tree life, the Sun★, the Moon★, the Stars★, all life forms in the oceans, birds, all cattle, beasts and creeping things and finally Man, who was created in Gods image. **Gen 1:5-31**

★The creation of the Sun, Moon and Stars, occurred at the **Gen 1:1** timeframe and the mention of them here is to identify and decree their use in the overall scheme of God's creation. This reference is similar to the reference to the creation of Man in **Gen 2:7**, we know God did not create Man at that time chronologically, it is simply a recapping of what occurred chronologically in **Gen 1:26**

The Gap Theory supports an old earth/universe and the Gap Theory also supports a six 24 hour day creation week account, eliminating the need to be associated with the atheistic view of evolution, as well as not being painted into a corner because of a young earth view. The Gap Theory then provides a way out of this dilemma and provides the true view of the origin of the universe. And so the Gap Theory accommodates a condition whereby the Christian no longer needs to face ridicule by the scientific community, nor do they have to be tainted by the ungodly evolution world view. They can hold their head high by walking in the truth.

I realize that there are a lot of Christians that want to hold on to the 6000 year young earth view and are resistant to the Gap Theory. But no matter the amount of "God said it and I believe it" attitude will change the fact that the external evidence does not support a 6000 year old earth/universe.

This was not a big issue 150 years ago when the scientific community did not have the influence it has now, 150 years ago Theology was the Queen of the sciences, the theological world view reigned supreme and there was no need to worry about witnessing to people that were skeptical because of the theory of evolution.

But times have changed, today if you try to witness to someone that is aware of the evidence of a much older earth, they are going to have difficulty with your young earth position and this person is not going to be swayed by your "God said it and I believe it" explanation.

And of course the preceding study I believe has proven beyond the shadow of a doubt that the Gap Theory is the correct understanding of the origin of the universe.

The above example of the more enlightened person, when witnessing to this person using the Gap Theory explanation regarding the origin of the universe has a much better chance to embrace the truth of this view and be open to the rest of what God says in His word about the plan of salvation.

Chapter 5

CONCLUSION

Today there are a lot of young people who were raised in the Church, who after they go to College, and are introduced to a secular world view dominated by the theory of evolution, which in today's higher education is no longer considered a theory, but instead is taught as scientific fact, and a student who dares to express a Christian world view is ridiculed and is tempted to leave the Church, because when they go back to their Christian Church leaders, in many cases they are told that a 6000 year old earth/universe view is what the Bible teaches.

In most instances when they go back to College "Armed" with that explanation, they are overwhelmed with scientific evidence showing a much older universe. It is not fair to our children to send them out among wolves with little or no defense for their faith and all because we have adopted a world view that is in error. The error of a young earth or the error of a "Christian, wannabe" evolution scheme. It is the equivalent of telling our children that the earth is flat and that they should simple accept it, because "God said it; I believe it and that settles it." It won't be long before these children will simple "drop out", and the little Christian faith they try to hang on to, will soon extinguish all together, unless we do something. We need to fight back, we need to equip and arm our children with the truth, and the Gap Theory will accomplish that.

The Gap Theory not only teaches the truth about the origin of the universe, it also **"Bridges the Gap"** (pardon the pun) between the 6000 year young earth world view and the pseudo "Christian" evolution world view.

Here is another way to look at it.

If we assumed that the Gap Theory was wrong and was not the correct view of the origin of the universe, and if we embrace the Gap Theory anyway, what harm will we have done? Do we dishonor God? Does it affect our salvation? Are we saying that God is **not** the creator like evolution does, or are we making God less of a God like Atheistic evolution and "Christian" evolution does, because they require that God has to be "put in a box" and use an evolutionary process in order to "create?"

The answer is **NO** to all this; the God of the Gap Theory is the same God as the God of the young (6000 year) earth theory.

The God of the Gap Theory still created the universe out of nothing, He still created (we would call it re-created) the earth in 6, 24 hour days and **rested** on the 7th 24 hour day.

The God (if you can call it that) of evolution and the God of the "Christian, wanabe evolution" did not speak and it came into being.

Atheistic evolution believes in a "Big Bang" theory, just not in a God behind the "Big Bang" theory,

"Christian" evolution believes in a "Big Bang" theory, their God just isn't Big enough to not need those silly 6 ages, millions or billions of years in duration in stead of six, 24 hour days.(I am sorry for calling this silly, but to me the whole evolutionary premise seems silly both the secular and the so called "Christian", they just try so hard to keep God out of the picture and doesn't the scripture say that "The wisdom of this world is foolishness with God")

The point here is the Gap Theory does **NOT** take away anything from the God of creation.

The Gap Theory simply puts the origin of the universe into the proper perspective, and says look, God created the universe out of nothing, He just did it in stages where:

1) He created the universe and the earth, **after that** there was a period of time (not evolution), just time in which the universe and the earth existed in a perfect and final state

2) **After that**, sin entered the perfect universe as the result of Satan's fall, which put a curse on the universe and in particular the earth which existed then, and the result upon the earth was that it became "without form and void, and darkness was upon the face of the deep." In addition to the physical curse upon the earth, another consequence of Satan's fall was the death of whatever creatures God had created at the Gen

1:1 time frame and whom we believe were under the charge of Lucifer (what he was called then but now he is better known as Satan) among those creatures we believe to be Dinosaurs and other prehistoric animals as well as a pre-Adamic race or host of Beings who were the source and origin of Demons and of whom Lucifer was in charge, these Beings fell because Satan fell in similar fashion as "death passing on all mankind" because of Adam's sin

3) **After that**, God re-created the earth over a six, 24 hour day period of time in which He created light, day, night, the firmament, the oceans (seas), the dry land, vegetation and tree life, the Sun, the Moon, The Stars, all life forms in the oceans, birds, cattle, beasts, and creeping things, and finally Man.

4) **After that**, Man sinned and we know the rest of that story.

The point is that the Gap Theory does not change or take away anything from Christian Theology Proper.

If the Gap Theory is truth (as we believe it is) then it adds a positive dimension to the Christian faith, and it equips the 21st century Christian with the tools he/she needs to contend for the "faith once delivered unto the saints" and equips the Christian to give an answer to "The hope that is in us, which is Christ in you the hope of glory"

Jude 3-Col 1:27

Made in the USA
Monee, IL
29 September 2021